Swear Word Coloring Book

BLACK PAPER EDITION

30 sweary designs
Swearing for Fun and Relaxation

THIAGO ULTRA

Swear Word Coloring Book - Black Paper Edition - 30 Sweary Designs: Swearing for Fun and Relaxation

Copyright 2017 by Thiago Ultra

ISBN-13: 978-1544245737
ISBN-10: 1544245734

All rights reserved. No portion of this book may be reproduced in any form without the written permission of the author. Colored pages of the illustrations presented in this book may not be used in any commercial form.

First edition, 2017

Artwork by Thiago Ultra

More about Thiago's books:
www.thiagoultra.com
www.facebook.com/tultra

Curse First, Color Later.

Zero Fucks Given

Piss Off

Prick

Sugartits

Bastard

Go to hell

Fucknugget

Asshat

Kiss my ass

Fuck that shit

Douche Bag

Slut

Dickhead

Dipshit

Fuck Off

Made in the USA
Las Vegas, NV
09 September 2022